Digging in a Gold Mine, with a Diamond Shovel

By

Dr. Darryl L. Claybon

Kindling the Flames of
The Entrepreneurial Spirit

Managers instruct,

Leaders inspire! Prof Casey Bethel

For centuries, the management model theories have been essentially the same. Managers are expected to be leaders. However, in modern times, the two are not necessarily synonymous. Managers understand the business: inventory, capital, accounting, forecasting, payroll, taxes, etc. Leaders understand the business, but also understand the employees and customers with whom they do business.

Is there is a need for a 21st century model of management? How does this model look? How does one manage multigenerational expectations with cutting edge technology?

Digging in a Gold Mine with a Diamond Shovel provides us with some possible answers.

Copyright Page

Digging in a Gold Mine with a Diamond Shovel
by Dr. Darryl L Claybon

Acknowledgements

To All: Thank you for all that you have invested, given, and poured into me. I never would have made it without you...

To my students: Thank you for the moments when the student became the teacher and this teacher became the student.

Dr. Darryl L. Claybon earned his Doctorate in Psychology of Religion concentrating in Personality Development. He served several years as a Corporate Banker, and now spends his life as a Professor in both online and campus classes. He has been intricately involved in leadership for over thirty years. He has a hands-on working knowledge of the complexities and intricacies of Business and Philosophy that can help guide the novice as well as the seasoned leader.

The Gold Mine represents the Marketplace.

The Diamond Shovel represents those who are asked "What do you bring to the table?" Their response: I bring the table! (Unknown)

The Square Head Shovels represent the New Millennium Workers and Technology.

The Owner represents the Modern Day Corporation

The Yard Worker & Family represent the New Corporation of the twenty-first century.

Dr. Darryl L. Claybon

Table of Contents

Managers Instruct, Leaders Inspire!

DIGGING IN A GOLD MINE, WITH A DIAMOND SHOVEL

The Diamond Shovel:

Revered, admired, and desired by many, however only possessed by one.

The System

The story is told of a man who possesses a diamond shovel. It is not clear how the man gains possession. Perhaps the man is born under a good sign, or maybe even a bad sign.

The Diamond Shovel is exquisite. It is beautiful beyond measure and imagination. The diamonds were formed and buried in the deepest part of the Garden of Eden. It is approximately five feet long with a diamond grip on the end. The shaft is long and elegant reflecting at any angle the joy of material abundance. The blade is rounded and pointed providing the holder with the unyielding comfort of the best that this world has to offer. Revered, admired, and desired, by all, however only possessed by one.

"Everyone has the innate, intuitive, & instinctive, ability to find gold!"

Unfortunately, not everyone uses their innate, intuitive, & instinctive ability to find gold...

The Diamond Shovel is unique. It has the power to tell the owner where to find gold. If the owner is willing to listen, gold that is pressed down, shaken together and full of good measure can be found. The Diamond Shovel instructs the man to start digging in his back yard. The man readily agrees and begins to dig, striking gold with the very first shovel full of dirt. Wheelbarrow after wheelbarrow the man hauls gold into his garage.

It is not long until the man has enough gold to buy some more land and a bigger facility to hold the gold. The Diamond Shovel points out the area, and the man buys it. Again, with the first shovel of dirt into the earth, and every shovel full from that point, the new land yields gold. As he continues to dig, he finds a gold mine on his new property. Indeed, a very fortunate man.

"If you do not have a dream, someone will hire you for minimum wage to build theirs."

The man takes the Diamond Shovel home every night. He washes the shovel with the best diamond cleaner that money can buy. He gently blow-dries the diamond with de-carbonized air. Then finally, using measured, alternating, butterfly strokes, he wipes the Diamond Shovel down with imported Chinese silk and wraps it in Egyptian wool. He places it in a hand crafted Cedars-of-Lebanon wooden case and put it in the Golden Greece Room for safe keeping. Indeed a fortunate man.

CEO: I brought you in the office today because I wanted you to hear this from me first:

" The company is moving in a new direction…"

System Failure

One day, the owner notices that the rounded, pointed blade of the Diamond Shovel allows some of the gold crumbs to fall to the earth. It disturbs the owner that the Diamond Shovel appears to be leaving some of the precious gold behind. In today's contemporary corporate society, we would say the Diamond Shovel is "leaving money on the table." The owner becomes even more agitated, as he starts to count the crumbs. As a matter of fact, he focuses more so on the bits that are left behind, than each shovel full of gold. The crumbs left behind are almost equal to the gold.

"If you do not have a plan, people will make plans for you!"

The owner develops a new strategy. He decides to take the company in a new direction. He determines that he will get the crumbs as well. The next day, he brings a larger square head shovel to work with him. He begins digging and true enough, the larger square head shovel, picks up the gold as well as the crumbs. The owner then begins to invest in more shovels that have the flat head. Even though the flat head shovels were not as durable as the Diamond Shovel, the owner continues to buy them.

For those that have not received the memo:

It is always darkest, just before the dawn...

Whatever can and will go wrong, will go wrong...

When it rains, it pours...

At one point, he even stops taking the Diamond Shovel to work with him. He no longer cleans it and even leaves it outside in the garage. To make room for the new shovels, he puts the Diamond Shovel, out back, in the cold, wet, dark, and nasty shed.

The Diamond Shovel spends a lot of time in the dark, dim, and gloomy shed. It begins to question its existence. In the shed the existential discussion begins: Why am I here? What is my purpose? Perhaps I was born at the wrong time, in the wrong place, and in the wrong world. Why is it I never seem to fit in or become comfortable? What did I do that was so wrong, there is no forgiveness? If this is my lot, perhaps it may have been better to have never been born at all….
How can a loser ever win?

Intelligent Design:

The System has a built-in self-correcting mechanism.

The System will correct itself!

(Dr. H. Allah)

The owner continues to build his wealth. He has more wealth than he or his children will ever spend. He continues to use only the new shovels.

Then, to make matters even worse, one night a storm comes and knocks over a tree that falls on top of the shed. Crushing the roof of the shed and allowing the rain to pour into the shed. It is a terrible night, not fit for man or beast. It rains as never before. The ruin of the shed, the house, and the land is tremendous. Everything is lost.

" Your hard work and contributions may appear to have gone unnoticed…"

The next morning at sunrise, the yard worker notices the fallen shed. As the yard worker approaches, he sees a small incredible sparkle under the rubbish. He draws near and tries to dig out what he believes is a little diamond in the rough. The rain, the mud, the rubbish, and the debris are covering the Diamond Shovel in such a way that only a small sparkle is visible. The yard worker tries and tries, but cannot seem to free what appears to be this little fantastic sparkling stone.

It is never too late to re-orchestrate the symphony called our life! (Back to School Mom-Lifetime Movie)

As the yard worker works feverishly, it is to no avail. The yard worker sits on the stump of the tree that has fallen. It is then that the Diamond Shovel begins to speak to the yard worker. "Since you tried to rescue me, you shall be rewarded. I will tell you where to find gold." The yard worker listens to the Diamond Shovel very carefully. He completes the instructions, and he finds gold.

The yard worker returns with some of the gold that he finds. He says, "Thank you for telling me where to find gold. However, I have brought some of the gold back to you." The Diamond Shovel says, "Since you have done this, now go and tell your family and friends where to find gold. " The yard worker says, "No, this is not fair, why should I prosper and you have no chance of escape?" The Diamond Shovel says, "Please allow me to bring joy to your life!" The yard worker tells his wife and children first. Then he tells the other members of his family and all of their friends. They all become wealthy beyond their wildest dreams.

Managers crash & burn,

Causing others to burn in the flames with them....

Leaders, like the Legendary Phoenix,

Not only

"Rise from the Ashes" But put out the fire, so others will not have to burn....

Then on the third day, the wife of the yard worker says to her husband, "We cannot leave it there, you must go back and retrieve "the talking diamond." How can I do this?" he asks. She replies "let us take our wealth and purchase the land."

The yard man agrees knowing it will take everything they have to buy the real estate. They purchase the land and go to retrieve what is believed to be "a talking diamond." However, to their discovery after digging in the earth, they find the Diamond Shovel.

The Diamond Shovel then opens a company that teaches others how to have wealth for their children and their children's children.

Lesson 1 from the Gold Mine:

The Diamond Shovel can lose its position.

Companies are in business to make a profit. The mission of the business is to maximize profits and minimize costs.

Lesson 2 from the Gold Mine:

The Diamond Shovel can lose its focus.

After losing its position and spending time in the dark places of life, the Diamond Shovel loses its focus. It questions its purpose and existence.

Lesson 3 from the Gold Mine:

However, the Diamond Shovel never loses its gift.

After being replaced and put aside. The gift within remains and the Diamond Shovel rises from the ashes. It starts a company that contributes to the life and welfare of its employees.

irony[1]

[ahy-ruh-nee]
noun, plural ironies.
1. the use of words to convey a meaning that is the opposite of its literal meaning:

the irony of her reply, "How nice!" when I said I had to work all weekend.
2.
Literature.

1. A technique of indicating, as through character or plot development, an intention or attitude opposite to that which is actually or ostensibly stated.

2. (Especially in contemporary writing) a manner of organizing a work so as to give full expression to contradictory or complementary impulses, attitudes, etc., especially as a means of indicating detachment from a subject, theme, or emotion.

Case Study 1

The Business Owner

The Owner of the shovel appears to be very greedy. He loses interest in the shovel and treats the shovel in a derogatory way. He begins to focus on the crumbs.

Imagine being the owner of a company. An employee starts the work week on Monday. The employee is supplied with everything needed to generate $99,000.00 by the end of the week. However, the employee only shows up with $69,000.00 in revenue. The employee worked five consecutive days. The employee was not late, nor impaired by health or ailments. The employee just shows up $30,000.00 short, saying "I did not bother with the crumbs."

The employee loses **$30, 000.00 weekly.**

The one employee loses **$120,000.00 monthly.**

The one employee loses **$1,360,000.00 annually.**

1 What would be your immediate response? Will this person continue to be on your payroll? Why/Why not?

2 "We have decided to take the company in a new direction." -What happens if a corporation does not evolve, embrace technology, or change with the times?

3 As a leader, describe how you would incorporate a growth strategy with this person?

Case Study 2

The Diamond Shovel

It appears the owner mistreats the Diamond Shovel. The owner no longer values the Diamond Shovel but places it in a dark and damp shed.

Employee A worked very hard for the company for many years. He was the top salesman for most of those years and was often referred to as "a rising star." He contributed substantially to the bottom line each and every quarter.

However, because of the economy, the company began layoffs and cutbacks. His department was the first to receive the layoffs. He was outraged. He left town to spend the weekend with his dad. He explained to his father saying, "They told me that I was an EFP (employee full of potential). They even put me in a specialized training program. "

His father was sympathetic to his son's quandary. Looking into the night sky, his father asks, "son do you know the difference between a rising star and a shooting star? The son looks puzzled. The father says "not much, they both end up burning out, and each one becomes a falling star! The law of gravity says that what goes up, at some point, sooner or later, must come down. Did you think the good times would last forever?"

1 "We have decided to take the company in a new direction" is not a bad situation, or is it? For the employee, how can it be positive?

2 Should the Diamond Shovel have prepared for rainy days?

3 As a leader, describe how you would design and incorporate a growth strategy for this employee, yourself and others for the rainy days?

Case Study 3
The Flat Head Shovels

The next day, he brings a larger square head shovel to work with him. He begins digging and true enough, the larger square head shovel, picks up the gold as well as the crumbs. The owner then begins to invest in more shovels that have the flat head. Even though the flat head shovels were not as durable as the Diamond Shovel, the owner continued to buy them.

Diane recently graduated from the University with honors. She is a quick learner, bright, intelligent, and embraces change. Diane exhibits the five keys to success every day: dresses well, reads well, writes well, listens well, and speaks well (Claybon, 2015). She is an employer's dream come true.

However, Diane's long term strategy includes working for the company a maximum of 24 months. Just like many millennials, she is building her resume, as opposed to coveting a gold retirement watch. She is only using the company as a stepping stone to her dream. She wants to own a Fortune 500 company.

1. Why is the turnover rate for millennials greater than those of the baby boomer generation?

2. Does Diane have a good strategy? Why or why not?

3. As a leader, how would you design and implement a growth strategy for Diane? How would you maximize her potential while she is at the company?

Case Study 4
The Yard Worker

The next morning at sunrise, the yard worker notices the fallen shed. As the yard worker approaches, he sees a small incredible sparkle under the rubbish.

Sam is an excellent employee but is little rough around the edges. He is not the top salesman in the branch yet very consistent in terms of reaching monthly and quarterly goals. He is not proficient in all five keys to success. Sam does not always, dress well, read well, write well, or speak well.

However, the manager notices that Sam listens well. In staff meetings, Sam can listen and empathize with others. At the branch he is known as the problem solver. He is very passionate about the company and can inspire others to see the big picture and connect the dots. During the time of policy changes, Sam can embrace and incorporate the changes quickly. Even though it is not in his job descriptions, he has the unique ability to puts out fires before they get started, and calm other employees' fears.

The manager calls Sam into the office, and promotes him to assistant manager.

1. **Did the manager do the right thing? Why or why not?**

2. **What would you call the ability "to put out fires and calm other employee fears?" How valuable is that employee?**

3. **As a leader, how would you design and incorporate a growth strategy for Sam?**

Recommended Reading

Carnegie, D. (1981). *How to win friends and influence people*. New York: Simon and Schuster

Dweck, C.S., & Gavin, M. (2013). Mindset: The New Psychology of Success: How We Can Learn to Fulfill Our Potential. New York: Your Coach Digital

Johnson, S. (1998). *Who moved my cheese?: An amazing way to deal with change in your work and in your life*. New York: Putnam

Sun-tzu, ., & Griffith, S. B. (1964). *The art of war*. Oxford: Clarendon Press.

Selah